THE BHAGAVAD GITA

A SELECTION

RAMESH S. BALSEKAR

Books by Ramesh S. Balsekar

- A Duet of One (2011)
- Dharma Se Swadharma Tak (Hindi 2011)
- Pursue 'Happiness' And Get Enlightened (2008)
- Celebrate the Wit & Wisdom: Relax and Enjoy (2008)
- Pointers From Ramana Maharshi (2008)
- Koun Parvah Karto?! (Marathi 2008)
- Does The Human Being Have Free Will? (2007)
- Enlightened Living (2007)
- A Buddha's Babble (2006)
- A Personal Religion of Your Own (2006)
- The Essence of The Ashtavakra Gita (2006)
- The Relationship Between 'I' And 'Me' (2006)
- A Homage To The Unique Teaching
  of Ramesh S. Balsekar (2006)
- Seeking Enlightenment – Why ? (2005)
- Nuggets of Wisdom (2005)
- The End of The Seeking (2005)
- Spiritual Search Step By Step (2004)
- Confusion No More (2003)
- Guru Pournima (2003)
- Upadesa Saram (2001)
- It So Happened That... (2000)
- Sin and Guilt: Monstrosity of Mind (2000)
- Meaningful Trivialities from the Source (2000)
- The Infamous Ego (1999)
- Who Cares?! (1999)
- The Essence of the Bhagavad Gita (1999)
- Your Head in the Tiger's Mouth (1997)
- Consciousness Writes (1996)
- Consciousness Strikes (1996)
- Consciousness Speaks (1995)
- Ripples (1994)

THE BHAGAVAD GITA
A SELECTION

RAMESH S. BALSEKAR

Copyright © 1995 Ramesh S. Balsekar

PUBLISHED BY

ZEN PUBLICATIONS
62, Juhu Supreme Shopping Centre,
Gulmohar Cross Road No. 9, JVPD Scheme,
Juhu, Mumbai 400 049. India.

Tel: +91 22 32408074
eMail: zenpublications@gmail.com
Website: www.zenpublications.com

CREDITS
Cover & Book Design by Red Sky Designs, Mumbai

ISBN 10 81-88071-18-8
ISBN 13 978-81-88071-18-0

PRINTED BY
Repro India Limited

The Basic Understanding

∿

THE basic perennial principle behind all religions (before they were corrupted by interpretations and formal rituals) was the same: the existence of a Reality, by whatever name called – Reality, Totality, Consciousness, God or whatever – which "never did not exist from the beginning of the human race".

This Reality, which the first human being must have experienced, is the awareness of BEING – I AM – before any thought could have occurred. This reality – I AM – got clouded through subsequent thinking based on the feeling of a personal identity.

The presence or absence of the sense of personal doership and achievement would thus seem to be the dividing line between the happening of the experience of Reality or its not happening.

What is the one single basis of the perennial principle? It is this: all there is, is Consciousness – impersonal Consciousness in the awareness "I am" – other than which, nothing exists. Impersonal Consciousness is immanent in every single object in the universe. Consciousness thus exists in all objects, both sentient and insentient.

While Consciousness merely exists in the insentient objects, it is through the sentient objects that Consciousness functions. In order to appreciate the full significance of this fact – that Consciousness functions through the sentient objects – it is necessary to realize completely that it is Consciousness which is the functioning principle in all human beings. You might quite easily substitute "God" for "Consciousness".

One more step takes us to the core of the understanding: If Consciousness (or God) is all that exists and functions through human beings, how can there ever arise the question of "personal" achievement for any human being? The supreme will of only one supreme power must prevail: Is it God's Will, or is it your will, that must prevail?! It is this basic principle on which must rest all spiritual quest: Consciousness is all there is – other than Consciousness, nothing is. The total and absolute acceptance of this basic principle must surely shatter all conventional spiritual patterns and also all ethical and religious formalism. And this is where religions differ – and thereby veer away from the perennial principle. At the same time, the total acceptance of the perennial principle – the total acceptance of What Is at any present moment – brings about a tremendous sense of total freedom. It can be translated as "Faith in God", in its truest and purest sense.

At this point a valid relevant question would arise: Even if I totally accept that it is Consciousness which functions through each and every physical organism, I cannot get rid of the actual feeling of being a separate individual with my own life to live. If I have no volition, and it is Consciousness which functions through my body, how do I live my life? How do I make decisions which I must make every day?

The answer is, in a way, simple. You act as if you are playing a role in the drama of life and living. You make decisions as and when you have to make them, *as if* you have the volition to make such decisions – with the deepest conviction that

Consciousness has already made those decisions along with their consequences. In this way, the man of understanding does not shirk making decisions, if making decisions is what he is supposed to do in playing the role which Consciousness has assigned to him. He thus makes his decision diligently, weighing the various alternatives, but knowing that it is Consciousness (or God) who is the actual functioning element, he does not have a feeling either of pride (if the action is successful) or feeling of failure or guilt (if the action turns out to be unsuccessful). In other words, he lives in the present moment; he does not live for that which is always out of reach, he does not live in servitude, thirsting for survival in the future, because he is convinced that the future is not in his hands.

Trust in God – acceptance of Consciousness as the ultimate reality in the functioning of the universe – makes life simple for the man of understanding. In the absence of a personal sense of doership the man of understanding does not engage in a self conscious and deliberate campaign to "do his duty" with the intention of acquiring happiness. Indeed he has come to the conviction that the whole concept of happiness and unhappiness is based on the world of objects and is thus in effect quite illusory and transitory.

The understanding that Consciousness (or God) is in charge of the functioning of the universe brings with it the simple good and the virtuous with which one is endowed by the very fact of being conscious – I AM. "I am" is reality. "I am so-and-so" is false, which brings with it the delusion of a sense of personal doership.

With this "Trust in God", grows quietly the humility and simplicity of ordinary life of faith, which is a matter of seeing the good as it exists – the What Is – rather than as something to be achieved through one's own effort. This happens as the result of the understanding that, as the Buddha has put it, there are events and deeds but no individual doer thereof. If there is no individual doer – and all actions are part of the functioning of Totality (or God's actions) – then my actions are not my own. More important, the actions of someone else are not his or her actions either – and therefore how can I consider anyone my enemy? With this basic understanding arises, naturally and spontaneously, humility, love and compassion. These are not virtues to be deliberately acquired – they cannot be acquired by personal effort. They

9

are a gift from God which come as a result of the simple, basic understanding.

The man of understanding is not really the man who has "by a lifetime of study and practice accumulated a great fund of virtue and merit", but the man in whom nature acts without the impediment of personal effort and vanity.

It is important to note that a contemplative life of meditation and interior awareness of himself would make the seeker as much obsessed with his self-improvement as the life of active effort and achievement. The true tranquility can only arise when there is the deepest conviction that there cannot be any self-will – that it is only God's will that must prevail all the time everywhere – and therefore the only thing to "do" is accept What Is, without wanting to change it and without wanting to become what one is not. The action of the man of understanding is not inaction but non-action from the personal point of view. The understanding itself becomes this non-action which transcends the distinction between action and inaction, the distinction between activity and contemplation or meditation. In other words, it is the understanding itself that brings about the union with the impersonal Consciousness or Totality or God.

It is necessary to emphasize that the proof of the arrival of understanding is an essential humility – "not the humility of virtuousness and conscious self-abasement, which in the end is never entirely free from the unctuousness of Uriah Heep, but the basic, one might say 'ontological' or 'cosmic' humility of the man who fully realizes his own nothingness and becomes totally forgetful of himself, "like a dry tree stump...like dead ashes."

Non-action or natural spontaneous action – is by no means inertia or quietism or fatalism. It is not mere passivity. On the contrary, non-action being both effortless and spontaneous, is in perfect accordance with our nature and with our place in the universal scheme of things. It is therefore free from force and violence, and, for that very reason is extraordinarily effective.

— *Excerpted from Ramesh S. Balsekar's* Ripples

∾

देहिनोऽस्मिन्यथा देहे कौमारं यौवनं जरा ।
तथा देहान्तरप्राप्तिर्धीरस्तत्र न मुह्यति ॥

The in-dwelling Consciousness in a body-mind organism passes through the stages of childhood, youth and old age. Similarly the same in-dwelling Consciousness, at the death of a body, passes on to another body. The wise one is not concerned with this phenomenon.

ॐ

THE in-dwelling Consciousness, referred to in the verse as *dehinah*, is the impersonal Consciousness which is the same life source in every living creature. This impersonal Consciousness is not concerned with the various stages in life through which the body-mind organism passes as a natural process. Nor is it concerned with the process beyond death, when it gives up one body and enters into another conception, another body.

It is the identified consciousness, the ego, which is very much concerned not only with the various stages in life – especially the loss of youth and the approach of old age – but also beyond death, the fear of the unknown.

❧

मात्रास्पर्शास्तु कौन्तेय शीतोष्णसुखदुःखदाः ।
आगमापायिनोऽनित्याः तांस्तितिक्षस्व भारत ॥

*Feelings of heat and cold, pleasure and pain, are
the result of the contact of the senses with their
respective objects. They are ephemeral, they come
and they go. All you should do is to accept them
as such without getting involved in them.*

ॐ

IT is clear that external objects bring about
a reaction in a body-mind organism only when
they come in contact with the respective senses. It
is also clear that the same object can bring about
different reactions in different human organisms.
What is attractive for one may not be attractive
to another. What seems attractive at one time may

also seem oppressive at another time. The point is that reactions of the senses to their respective objects are different and they keep changing; also, they come and go. When they are seen in this perspective, they lose their influence to cause undue pleasure or pain. One can accept the changes as they occur with equanimity.

❧

वासांसि जीर्णानि यथा विहाय
नवानि गृह्णाति नरोऽपराणि ।
तथा शरीराणि विहाय जीर्णानि
अन्यानि संयाति नवानि देही ॥

As a man casts off worn-out garments and dons
new ones, so the in-dwelling Consciousness casts
off worn-out body-mind organisms and enters
into new ones.

∾

THIS oft-quoted verse is very often grossly
misinterpreted as under:

"Just as an individual changes his clothes to
suit the convenience of the occasion, so too the
ego-centre discards one physical form and takes
to another, which will be most suited for it (to
gain the next required type of experiences)."

'*Dehi*' mentioned in the verse, refers not to the 'ego-centre' but to the in-dwelling Consciousness, the impersonal Consciousness which is the life source of all living creatures. It is this impersonal Consciousness which casts off worn-out body-mind equipments and enters into new ones as part of general evolution.

❧

अव्यक्तादीनि भूतानि व्यक्तमध्यानि भारत ।
अव्यक्तनिधनान्येव तत्र का परिदेवना ॥

Beings are not manifest to human senses before birth. During the period between birth and death they are manifest. They again return to the unmanifest at death. In this natural process what is there to grieve over?

∾

PERSONS and events appearing in one's dream did not exist before the dream started and will again disappear when the dream ends. No one grieves over this phenomenon. Why grieve over a similar phenomenon in life, in this living dream? This would seem to be the purport of this verse.

When the potential energy of the unmanifest activised itself into the manifest universe, the manifestation came into existence. When the burst of energy exhausts itself after billions of years, the manifested universe again subsides into the potential energy of the unmanifest – until it activises itself again. This is a perfectly natural process which should not be of any concern to the man of discernment.

Myriad forms of life emerge only to return to a primal non-being before entering again to some form of living – a kind of re-cycling. Thus nature would seem to be a rhythmic pulsation, ever-changing and transforming, coming to birth and dying and coming to birth again. Wisdom consists in learning conformity to the universal rhythm.

ॐ

देही नित्यमवध्योऽयं देहे सर्वस्य भारत ।
तस्मात्सर्वाणि भूतानि न त्वं शोचितुमर्हसि ॥

The in-dwelling Consciousness within all living body-mind organisms is forever invulnerable, indestructible. Therefore there is really no need to mourn for any one.

∾

IT is necessary to make a distinction – perhaps subtle but very necessary – between mourning for someone and reacting emotionally to the loss of a near relative or a dear friend. It is natural for the body-mind organism to react to the loss of someone who has been close to one, especially over a long period. While such a spontaneous reaction is perfectly natural, prolonged mourning or grieving over a period is a matter of involvement of the ego through identification with the body. In other words, while an emotional reaction is perfectly natural, an involvement is a matter of ignorance.

Ramana Maharshi was once greatly upset emotionally when a companion over a long period suddenly died. As an explanation he came out with a very similar view.

∾

नेहाभिक्रमनाशोऽस्ति प्रत्यवायो न विद्यते ।
स्वल्पमप्यस्य धर्मस्य त्रायते महतो भयात् ॥

In this Karma Yoga, *an attempt is not wasted even if it is an abortive one. Nor is there any adverse effect. Even a little knowledge and practice of this* Yoga *protects one from the great fear (of death and rebirth).*

ॐ

IN this verse, Lord Krishna brings out the difference between what happens in the phenomenal working of life and the transcendental effort. While the effort in usual life could be wasted or even bring about an adverse effect, that does not hold good for any effort made in the acquisition of the knowledge and practice of *Karma Yoga*. A partial effort in raising a crop would be wasted if the process is not duly completed. Also, if a patient takes the wrong medicine, there could be an adverse effect. But the practice of *Karma Yoga* is on a different footing altogether. The very wanting to undertake the *Karma Yoga* is because of God's Grace. So, the progress of the undertaking in the process would also depend on God's Grace. But the remarkable thing about this *Yoga* process is that nothing done is ever wasted, nor does it have any adverse effect. The process goes on – the speed of it will depend on the destiny of the individual organism, through which the process goes on.

❦

यावानर्थ उदपाने सर्वत: संप्लुतोदके ।
तावान्सर्वेषु वेदेषु ब्रह्मणस्य विजानत: ॥

*The Vedas are useful only until the awakening. To
the awakened sage – the* Brahmana – *the Vedas
are as useful as a reservoir when there is a flood
everywhere.*

∾

FOR the spiritual seeker, the Vedas are the
prime source of true knowledge and everyone
must go to the sacred book for knowledge, just as
the villager must normally go to the well for his
daily supply of drinking water. But when the area
is flooded, the reservoir itself becomes merged in
the spread of water around. Similarly the Vedas are
useful only until the seeker has reached a certain
level of understanding, only until the individual is
not free from the desire for sensual satisfaction.

But to the seeker who has come to experience *Brahman*, the *Brahmana*, the knowledge of the Vedas has become submerged in the perfection of the Self which the adept actually lives in practice.

∾

कर्मण्येवाधिकारस्ते मा फलेषु कदाचन ।
मा कर्मफलहेतुर्भू: मा ते सङ्गोऽस्त्वकर्मणि ॥

All you can do is to work for the sake of the work.
You have no right to the fruits of the work (the
consequences of your actions are not in your
control). But do not let this fact make you lean
towards inaction.

ॐ

THIS is one of the most quoted of the verses
in the *Bhagavad Gita*, and it is at the same time,
perhaps the most difficult to accept whole-
heartedly: how can the human being act without
motivation? And yet this is precisely what he is
asked to do!

The whole dilemma is based on the

misconception that if a man is asked to work without expecting the fruit of his action, he would be inclined not to work. The misunderstanding is based on the belief that a human being has the free will to act or not to act.

Nobody likes being told that he has no free will. And yet look at the state of the world at the present time. The world is on the brink of disaster, where it has been for many years now with one crisis after another. The question – the big question – therefore remains: The human being certainly has tremendous intelligence (to send a man to the moon); he is also supposed to have free will – then why has the human being been unable to combine his intelligence and his free will to make the world a better place?!

There is also another aspect. There are so many intelligent people, leaders in their respective fields, who are very much interested in knowing their future. If they really believed in their own free will, why would they be so interested in astrology and similar phenomena?!

If you think along these lines, the only reasonable conclusion you will arrive at is that the human being has been acting in this fashion because he has no control over his thoughts and emotions. What he considers as *his* actions are in fact only *reactions* of the individual organism to an outside impulse: a thought which occurs, an event that he sees or perhaps what he happens to hear. Each organism reacts according to the natural characteristics with which it has been programmed: physical, mental, intellectual, temperamental.

Another difficulty about truly accepting this teaching is the argument that it leads to a "fatalistic" attitude. The fatalistic argument translates itself into the question: if I am not to be motivated by the fruits of my action, and, indeed, if I have no free will over my actions, why should I work at all? The answer is astonishingly simple: you will not be able to be inactive for any length of time because the energy within the organism will compel you to act; to act according to the natural characteristics of the organism. In other words, whether to act not is itself not in your control.

❧

या निशा सर्वभूतानां तस्यां जागर्ति संयमी ।
यस्यां जाग्रति भूतानि सा निशा पश्यतो मुने : ॥

In the knowledge of the Atman, *which is the dark night to the ignorant, the recollected mind is fully awake and aware. The ignorant are awake in the daylight of their sense-life, which is darkness to the sage.*

∾

IN this verse are contrasted the view of the world as seen by the identified individual and that of the awakened *jnani*. To the ignorant individual whatever is seen by the senses appears real and is taken as real – and only that which is perceived through the senses is real. To the sage, on the other hand, whatever appears is not real: whatever appears is only the changeable appearance of the unperceived Real. In other words, the ego-centric, identified individual, fully awake to the world of perception, is asleep to the real, the *Atman*, lived and enjoyed by the sage. So long as the individual remains in his world of desires, the Real – the *Atman* – remains a total mystery to him. It is only when he realizes that the mind is nothing but a series of desires which never ends, that the possibility occurs of his awakening from the night of identification with the senses into the world of the *jnani*.

Ramana Maharshi said, "There are only two things: sleep and creation. There is nothing if you go to sleep; you wake up and there is everything. If you learn to 'sleep' when awake, you can be just a witness. This is the real truth."

∾

न कर्मणामनारम्भात् नैष्कर्म्य पुरूषोऽश्नुते ।
न च संन्यसनादेव सिद्धिं समधिगच्छति ॥

Abstaining from action is not the way to gain freedom from activity. Nor can one achieve perfection by merely ceasing to act.

∾

THIS verse makes a distinction between activity, inactivity and non-activity. Freedom from activity means not inactivity but the absence of sense of personal doership. Deliberate inactivity simply means activity in the negative sense and is at the same level as positive deliberate activity. When activity happens – because the energy within the body-mind organism will not permit the organism to remain idle for any length of time – then such activity is without the sense of

31

personal doership and may therefore be called not action nor inaction but non-action. Non-action is action without a sense of personal doership whereas both deliberate action and deliberate inaction include the sense of personal doership.

The essential difference between the kind of activity or lack of activity is whether the sense of personal doership is inherent in such activity or inactivity. It is the absence of the sense of personal doership which leads to perfection – and not the activity or inactivity as such.

The Chinese philosophy called Taoism puts this as under:

"The non-action of the wise man is not inaction. It is not studied. It is not shaken by anything. The sage is quiet because he is not moved, not because he *wills* to be quiet. The heart of the wise man is tranquil."

In other words, from the stillness of the sages comes their non-action which is indeed effective action because there is no ego involved in such non-action.

❧

न हि कश्चिक्षणमपि जातु तिष्ठत्यकर्मकृत् ।
कार्यते ह्यवश: कर्म सर्व: प्रकृतिजैर्गुणै: ॥

*Actually, not even for a moment can one remain
free of activity (including mental activity, both
conscious and subconscious). The energy within the
body-mind organism will automatically produce
actions according to the natural characteristics of
the organism.*

ॐ

THIS verse provides the answer to the usual
objection raised against the injunction to act
without expecting and wanting the fruits of action
– that such an injunction will lead to a "fatalistic"
attitude i.e. a person will have no reason to act
at all, and he would therefore be inclined not to
act at all. In other words, you may want to desist
from action if you cannot have the fruits of your

action. But the fact of the matter is that the fruits of the action will depend on the destiny of the organism, whereas the energy within the body-mind organism will continue to produce activity in accordance with the natural characteristics with which the organism was conceived and created. These natural characteristics depend on the genes – the DNA – of the organism and the conditioning that the organism has received from the environment in which it was raised. And the essential fact is that no one has the control either over the DNA or over the environment, in which the organism was born: no one can choose one's parents and, by the same token, no one can choose the environment in which one is born, and gets conditioned in.

❧

कर्मेन्द्रियाणि संयम्य य आस्ते मनसा स्मरन् ।
इन्द्रियार्थान्विमूढात्मा मिथ्याचार: स उच्यते ॥

*A man who renounces certain physical actions
but cannot control his mind from dwelling on the
objects of his sensual desire, is deceiving himself.
Such a man can only be called a hypocrite.*

ॐ

IT is a matter of fact that it is not very difficult
to restrain oneself from doing certain actions.
But it is far more difficult to restrain the mind
from thinking of the very activities which one has
forcibly deprived oneself. Continued practice of
such an attitude means self-delusion and such a
man is therefore soon known as a hypocrite. In
fact a hypocrite cannot help exposing himself
because the mind that cannot keep out sensuous

pleasures naturally assumes a tendency towards such actions and very soon the individual finds himself engaging in the very activities which he was trying forcibly to avoid.

❧

यस्त्वात्मरतिरेव स्यात् आत्मतृप्तश्च मानव: ।
आत्मन्येव च संतुष्ट: तस्य कार्य न विद्यते ।।

नैव तस्य कृतेनार्थ: नाकृतेनेह कश्चन ।
न चास्य सर्वभूतेषु कश्चिदर्थव्यपाश्रय: ।।

*A man is no longer obliged to perform any kind
of action, once he has learned to find delight and
satisfaction and peace in the Atman or Self.*

*For such a man there is nothing to gain in this
world by any kind of action; nor does he have
anything to lose by refraining from action. He is
independent of anybody and anything.*

෴

TO one who has transcended his ego, the
routine work during the day is no longer required

as self-discipline but is a natural fulfilment of his Self-realization. Such a man of Wisdom does not need to work in order to get his material requirements which go on increasing continuously for the ordinary man. He is perfectly content in the very Divine Nature – that provides eternal satisfaction for him. Where contentment has finally arrived in the very Self-realization, desires cannot arise, and in the absence of involvement in the desires there is no question of any action to satisfy the desires; nor are there any obligatory duties for such a Self-realized man because such duties concern only the man who has desires. Whatever work such a man does, just happens without any trace of doership.

Such a Self-realized man, rooted in the experience of the Self, does not have to depend for his satisfaction on any object or person because he is centred in the eternal subject.

∾

प्रकृते: क्रियमाणानि गुणै: कर्माणि सर्वश:।
अहङ्कारविमूढात्मा कर्ताहमिति मन्यते॥

तत्त्ववित्तु महाबाहो गुणकर्मविभागयो:।
गुणा गुणेषु वर्तन्त इति मत्वा न सज्जते॥

*It is the energy within the body-mind organism
that produces actions according to the natural
characteristics of the organism. Man, deluded by
his egoism, thinks "I am the doer."*

*But the one who has true insight into the working
of the energy within the organism, does not get
involved in the actions which are the result of the
senses attaching themselves to their respective
objects.*

ॐ

WHAT an ordinary person considers "his"
actions, are really reactions produced by the

brain in response to the senses when they meet their respective objects. Thus when the eyes see something or the ears hear something, the brain reacts to this event according to the natural characteristics of the body-mind organism, and produces a reaction. It is this natural reaction to the event which the ordinary man mistakenly considers his action.

The wise man, *Tattvavith* – who knows Reality – on the other hand, understands what really happens and does not involve himself with whatever happens. In other terms, the wise man considers all events as God's actions and therefore does not judge them as 'good' or 'bad'.

Ramakrishna Paramahaunsa gave his disciples this simple advice: "Be absolutely convinced that you are merely a machine which is operated upon by God, and then you may do whatever you want."

❧

सदृशं चेष्टते स्वस्या: प्रकृतेर्ज्ञानवानपि।
प्रकृतिं यान्ति भूतानि निग्रह: किं करिष्यति ॥

इन्द्रियस्येन्द्रियस्यार्थे रागद्वेषौ व्यवस्थितौ।
तयोर्न वशमागच्छेत् तौ ह्यस्य परिपन्थिनौ ॥

Even for a wise man, the energy within the body-mind organism produces actions according to his own natural characteristics. All living creatures follow their natural tendencies. What is the use of any external restraint?

The attraction and aversion of the senses for their respective objects are natural. Involvement with them should be avoided – that is the obstruction and obstacle.

ॐ

THIS verse makes it perfectly clear that the body-mind organism produces actions strictly

according to the natural character of that organism
– physical, mental, temperamental. And these
actions depend upon the destiny of that organism.
Once this is clearly understood, it will be realized
that, whether Self-realization has happened in
the organism or not, the body-mind organism
will react to an outside impulse – a thought or
something seen or something heard or something
smelt or touched – and the reaction will be strictly
according to the natural characteristics of that
organism. The only difference between the wise
man and the ordinary man lies in the reaction to
that reaction. Whilst the ordinary man will get
involved in the natural reaction, the wise man will
not: both the event and the reaction will be merely
witnessed without any personal involvement.

∾

श्रेयान् स्वधर्मो विगुण: परधर्मात्स्वनुष्ठितात् ।
स्वधर्मे निधनं श्रेय: परधर्मो भयावह: ॥

It is better to do one's own duty, however imperfectly, than to assume the duties of another, however successfully. It is better to die doing one's own duty: the duty of someone else will bring you into great spiritual danger.

∽

THE word '*dharma*' in Sanskrit has several meanings and the correct meaning has to be understood in context. Here, the words, "one's own duty" must mean the duty that is relevant to one's own natural characteristics. The duty – the *dharma* – of a flower is to bloom and emit its fragrance. While most of nature does its duty without any problem, a man's mind plays tricks on him and wants him to decide which *dharma* he will follow. If a man's natural characteristics are for a man to be an accountant, it would, the verse says, be suicidal to try to be a doctor or a lawyer for other reasons.

The verse is addressed to Arjuna and says to him, in effect: you are born to be a warrior; you are trained to be a warrior; your *dharma* is to fight, whether you win or lose, even if you die in doing your duty. Arjuna is hereby warned that if he tries to live the quiet and peaceful life of a Brahmin, that will be a great spiritual danger.

❧

वीतरागभयक्रोधाः मन्मया मामुपाश्रिताः ।
बहवो ज्ञानतपसा पूता मभ्दावमागताः ॥

*Freed from lust, fear and anger, filled with Myself,
finding refuge in Me, burnt and purified in the
blaze of Wisdom, many have entered into My
Being.*

～

THIS verse provides considerable
encouragement to the seeker. It says that by
following any path that is appropriate to the
natural characteristics of the human organism –
the path of action, or the path of devotion, or the
path of knowledge – many have reached the final
truth, the Absolute. Lord Krishna assures Arjuna
that reaching the Absolute, the ultimate Being, is

not the almost impossible feat that it is generally made out to be. Whatever the path followed, it is necessary to lose the sense of doership, which means not getting involved in attachment, fear and anger. Ultimately, what counts is the faith and trust in God or the Impersonal Reality.

❧

कर्मण्यकर्म य: पश्येत् अकर्मणि च कर्म य: ।
स बुद्धिमान्मनुष्येषु स युक्त: कृत्स्नकर्मकृत् ॥

*He who sees the inaction that is in action, and the
action that is in non-action, is wise among men.
Even when engaged in action, he remains in the
equanimity of the Self.*

ॐ

THOSE who are caught in the machinery of
money and power take no joy except in activity and
change. Whenever an occasion for action arises,
they feel compelled to act: they cannot, in their
ignorance, help themselves. They are inexorably
moved, like the machine of which they are a part.
Prisoners in the world of phenomenality, what
else can they do but submit to the demands of
matter!

The heart of the wise man is tranquil. As a Taoist sage has put it:

"It is the mirror of heaven and earth, the glass of everything. Emptiness, stillness, tranquility, tastelessness, silence, non-action – this is the level of heaven and earth. This is perfect Tao. Wise men find here their resting place. Resting, they are empty."

It is from the sage's emptiness that stillness arises, and from stillness, action that is non-action.

ॐ

यस्य सर्वे समारम्भा: कामसङ्कल्पवर्जिता: ।
ज्ञानाग्निदग्धकर्माणं तमाहु: पण्डितं बुधा: ॥

*The sages say truly he is wise who acts without
lust or scheming for the fruit of the acts – the
acts do not affect him for they are melted in the
wisdom of My knowledge.*

∾

THIS verse again stresses the importance of
the sage's action that is so natural that it seems
like inaction: in reality it is action that is non-
action.

The Taoist sage has put it in the following
words:

*The man in whom Tao acts without impediment
Harms no other being by his actions.*

Yet he does not know himself
To be 'kind', to be 'gentle'.

The man in whom Tao acts without impediment
Does not bother with his own interests
And does not despise others who do.

He does not struggle to make money
And does not make a virtue of poverty.
He goes his way without relying on others
And does not pride himself on walking alone.

❧

ब्रह्मार्पणं ब्रह्म हवि: ब्रह्माग्नौ ब्रह्मणा हुतम् ।
ब्रह्मैव तेन गन्तव्यं ब्रह्मकर्मसमाधिना ॥

Brahman *is the ritual,* Brahman *is the offering,*
Brahman *is he who makes the offering to the*
fire that is Brahman. *If in every action, a man*
recognizes Brahman, *he will verily be absorbed*
into Brahman.

ॐ

THIS verse is chanted by Hindu monks as
"grace" before meals, the "fire" being regarded as
the fire of hunger, *jatharagni.*

The metaphor in this verse refers to the well-
known ritual of the Vedas i.e. the *Yajna.* In every
Yajna, there are four essential factors: a) the deity
invoked to whom the oblation is offered; b) the
fire in which the oblation is poured; c) the material

that constitutes the offering, and d) the individual who is performing the *Yajna*.

The significance of the chanting of the verse as "grace" before meals is that the consumption of food is a necessity for all, including the wise one. The point is that the wise one thinks of the act of consuming food as a *jnana-yajna*: the food, the eater of it, the digesting of it, are all modifications of *Brahman* just as the waves are part of the ocean.

❧

यत्साङ्ख्यै: प्राप्यते स्थानं तद्योगैरपि गम्यते ।
एक साङ्ख्य च योग च य: पश्यति स पश्यति ॥

*The wise ones who see knowledge and action as
one have the true understanding: either path leads
to the same end. There the followers of Karma-
yoga meet the seekers after knowledge in equal
freedom.*

∾

IN this verse Lord Krishna categorically
declares that neither the *Jnana-yoga* nor the
Karma-yoga (neither the path of knowledge nor
the path of Action) is the sole way to emancipation.
One can reach the goal by either path.

Most seekers want to know "the best path"
to salvation. This is a misconception based on
the erroneous belief that one's path is a matter of
choice. The fact of the matter is that one has not
chosen to be a seeker: one is a seeker because that

is his destiny and because God has willed it to be
so. The natural characteristics of the body-mind
organism – over which one has had no control
– decide what one shall seek. In other words, it
is God's Will that will decide whether one will
seek money and power, or salvation. The spiritual
seeker thus need not feel himself to be superior to
someone who is seeking material things.

To take the argument a step further, if the
seeking itself has not been a matter of our choice,
how can the path be a matter of our choice? Our
destiny and the natural characteristics of our body-
mind organisms will naturally dictate what path
we shall take. God's Will will direct us towards
the path we are to follow.

It is, therefore, a matter of great satisfaction
to the seeker that any path will lead to the same
goal.

नैव किञ्चित्करोमीति युक्तो मन्येत तत्त्ववित् ।
पश्यञ्शृण्वन्स्पृशञ्जिघ्रन् अश्नन्गच्छन्स्वपञ्श्वसन् ॥

प्रलपन्विसृजन्गृह्न् उन्मिषन्निमिषन्नपि ।
इन्द्रियाणीन्द्रियार्थेषु वर्तन्त इति धारयन् ॥

The sage centred in Brahman *has the constant,
underlying thought "I am doing nothing". He is
totally firm in the thought that the senses react to
the sense objects – no matter what he sees, hears,
touches, smells, eats. It matters not whether he is
moving, sleeping, breathing, speaking, excreting,
or grasping something with his hand, or opening
or closing his eyes: he knows that he is doing
nothing at all.*

॰

THIS verse emphasizes the fact that the essential feature of Self-awareness or Enlightenment or Awakening is the total annihilation of the sense of doership in whatever activity that is being produced through the body-mind organism.

Says Ramakrishna Paramahaunsa: "He who comes to know that he is only an instrument in the hands of the Lord, has no egoistic feeling. He is aware that he is only a tool with which God has His work done. Such a man causes harm to nobody. The poison of egoism is no more in him. A steel knife becomes a gold knife with the touch of the philosopher's stone. Though the form of the knife is there, it is not useful anymore for cutting. Similarly, the *jnani* retains a seeming individuality, but no ignorance-born activity occurs in and through him."

❧

नादत्ते कस्यचित्पापं न चैव सुकृतं विभु: ।
अज्ञानेनावृतं ज्ञानं तेन मुह्यन्ति जन्तव: ॥

The Omnipresent Lord does not take note of the merit or demerit of anyone. What-is is always perfect. The light of the Atman is covered by the darkness of delusion, and that is how the human beings are deluded.

∾

THIS verse firmly demolishes the concept of a God sitting somewhere in the clouds, peeping down and keeping a perfect account of every sin and every good deed done by every single human being, so that an individual may be punished or rewarded in due course. It should be clear that such a concept is steeped in ignorance. Such a concept cannot prevail if one is totally convinced that no action can happen except by God's Will. If

God's Will is totally accepted, one's personal will cannot exist, and therefore, there cannot be any question of any sin or merit.

Such a concept is bound to evoke immediately an argument such as this: if it is God's Will that I should commit a murder, why should I be punished for it?! The answer is astonishingly simple: there is no "you" to be punished or rewarded; it was God's Will, and the destiny of that human organism, that the murder would be committed, and it is also God's Will, and the destiny of that organism, to be punished for the act.

∾

बन्धुरात्मात्मनस्तस्य यैनात्मैवात्मना जित: ।
अनात्मनस्तु शत्रुत्वे वर्तेतात्मैव शत्रुवत् ॥

Man's will and intention is the only friend of the
Atman. *It is the same will and intention which acts*
as the enemy. For when a man is self-controlled,
his will acts as the friend of the Atman. *The same*
will of a man who has not subdued his base self,
acts like an enemy.

∽

THIS verse clearly brings out the influence
which the sense of personal doership has on the
psyche of the individual. To the extent that an
individual feels himself to be in control over his
destiny, that it is his free will which will dictate
his future in this world, his will and intention
– his mind – will be his enemy. The same mind
will be a friend to him who truly believes and
accepts that the only will that can prevail at any

time is God's Will, that he himself is merely an instrument operated upon by God. It is a matter of either a total surrender to God, or a strong sense of personal choice, personal doership and personal responsibility: one is knowledge, the other is ignorance.

∾

यो मां पश्यति सर्वत्र सर्वं च मयि पश्यति ।
तस्याहं न प्रणश्यामि स च मे न प्रणश्यति ॥

सर्वभूतस्थितं यो मां भजत्येकत्वमास्थित: ।
सर्वथा वर्तमानोऽपि स योगी मयि वर्तते ॥

*The Yogi who sees me in all things and all things
within me, will never lose sight of Me, nor do I
ever become lost to him.*

*He is established in union with Me, and worships
me devoutly as existing in all beings. Such a Yogi
always abides in Me, whatever may be his mode
of living.*

☙

WHAT this verse says in essence is that while
the universe appears as diversity, essentially all is
unicity, and it is the *Yogi* – the wise man – who

sees this truth behind the apparent universe, and thus becomes one with the unicity.

Noumenon and phenomena, potential energy and activised energy, thought and action are essentially one in unicity and are dual only in phenomenality. The ocean remains the same whether or not there are waves on its surface. It is as if the ocean sports with the waves in a sportive mood. Similarly energy activates its potentiality into the actuality of phenomenal life, but essentially they are not two. Unmanifest Noumenon, in a burst of love energy, becomes the phenomenal manifestation – life and living as we know it – but essentially there is only Unicity. When the love play is over – when the burst of energy is exhausted – the manifested phenomena merge with the unmanifest Noumenon in Unicity.

As the *Bhagavatam* puts it:

"As the spider weaves its thread out of its own mouth, plays with it and then withdraws it again into itself, so the external unchangeable Lord, who is without form, without attributes, who is absolute knowledge and absolute bliss, evolves the whole universe out of Himself, plays with it for a while, and again withdraws it into Himself."

The one who really sees this Truth, realizes his own nature as the Self.

❧

मनुष्याणां सहस्रेषु कश्चिद्यतति सिद्धये ।
यततामपि सिद्धानां कश्चिन्मां वेत्ति तत्त्वतः ॥

*It is perhaps only one in thousands of beings who
strives for freedom. And amongst those who strive
for freedom – and think they have succeeded –
hardly one knows the total Truth of My Being.*

ॐ

WITHOUT a certain innate God-given
intuitive insight, it is so easy to misunderstand
many verses in the *Bhagavad Gita*.

It is thus possible to misinterpret this verse as
Lord Krishna shifting the entire responsibility for
not realizing the Self upon the individual seeker
himself and attributing the failure to the seeker's
lack of self-application. But it must be realized
that whatever anyone seeks must be seen as the
seeking happening through an individual human

organism as its God-given destiny. Then it will be seen that there is truly no individual seeker who could be proud of being a spiritual seeker. If someone seeks money and power, it is because God wants him to do so. If a man seeks spirituality, again, it is because there is God's Grace.

This verse is to be seen as Lord Krishna stating the fact of the matter: how rare it is for someone to seek freedom and perfection, and how much rarer it is for someone to ultimately know the total Truth.

On the other hand, the Lord has already (IV/10) assured the seeker that "freed from lust, fear and anger, filled with Myself, finding refuge in Me, burnt and purified in the blaze of wisdom, *many have entered into My Being.*"

The point is that it is not every seeker who can aspire for total perfection. It is a matter of Divine Will: all he can do is to accept this Divine Will and not let his desire for freedom itself become an obstruction. What this means is that the seeker must surrender to God's Will in regard to the entire process of awakening. That he is a seeker is itself because of God's Grace: surrender to this Grace, and leave everything to that Will.

A similar encouragement is voiced by Ramana Maharshi when he tells the seeker: "Your head is already in the tiger's mouth, there is no escape." Why be impatient?!

∾

भूमिरापोऽनलो वायु: खं मनो बुद्धिरेव च ।
अहङर इतीयं मे भिन्ना प्रकृतिरष्टधा ।।

अपरेयमितस्त्वन्यां प्रकृतिं विद्धि मे पराम् ।
जीवभूतां महाबाहो ययेदं धार्यते जगत् ।।

My prakriti *is of eightfold composition: earth,
water, fire, air, ether, mind, intellect and the ego.
Bear this in mind that behind this – and quite
distinct from it – is That perennial principle which
is the source of life and the sustenance of the
universe – Consciousness in all beings.*

ॐ

THIS verse provides the distinction between
the manifest material universe and the perennial
principle which, immanent within it, provides the
life and the sustenance to this universe.

The material manifest universe is just a
sudden, spontaneous, concurrent appearance in

Consciousness, within Consciousness, brought about by Consciousness: Consciousness is all there really is. In the material manifestation, the human being is just one object; basically there is no difference in the make-up of the human being and the inanimate object. The question, therefore, of the individuality of the human being is really a myth.

In principle, therefore, the human being is merely a dreamed character in this dreamed manifestation – just another object – with senses which enable him to perceive things, and cognize and interpret and discriminate between what he perceives. If he sees the impersonality in all this, that he is just another object in the manifestation with certain additional endowments, like sentience and intellect, that would be the first step in perceiving the impersonality of the whole manifestation. In seeing the impersonality of the manifested universe, there is the inherent understanding that whatever has appeared as a mere appearance cannot possibly have any existence of its own, that Consciousness is the perennial principle which is the source of life and the sustenance of the universe.

∾

ये चैव सात्त्विकाभावा: राजसास्तामसाश्चं ये ।
मत्त एवेति तान्विद्धि न त्वहं तेषु ते मयि ॥

त्रिभिर्गुणमयैर्भावि: एभि: सर्वमिदं जगत् ।
मोहितं नाभिजानाति मामेभ्य: परमव्ययम ॥

*You must realize that anything that belongs to the
states of sattva, rajas and tamas, must proceed
from me: they are contained in me, but I am not
in them. It is by the moods and mental states – the
expression of these three gunas – that the entire
world is deluded. Thus the world fails to recognize
Me as I really Am: Supreme and deathless, I stand
apart from them all.*

☙

THE individual human body-mind mechanism
is really nothing but an individual pattern of
dynamic energy. That is all an individual is:

energy vibrating and pulsating at an incredible speed in a particular pattern. And that pattern has characteristics peculiar to that particular body-mind organism. No human being has natural characteristics quite like any other. The scriptures refer to this combination of characteristics as *dharma*, the original nature. Indeed, in another verse, Lord Krishna tells Arjuna to act according to his original nature: to follow one's *dharma* even imperfectly done is better than following another's *dharma* more efficiently. He adds that following someone else's *dharma* is spiritually dangerous.

The Arabian sage Monoimus says:

"Learn whence is sorrow and joy, and love and hate, and the waking though one would not and sleeping though one would not, and falling in love though one would not, and, if thou shouldst closely investigate all these phenomena, thou wilt find God in thyself one and many, just as the atom, thus finding in thyself a way out of thyself."

❧

बहुनां जन्मनामन्ते ज्ञानवान्मां प्रपद्यते ।
वासुदेव: सर्वमिति स महात्मा सुदुर्लभ: ॥

*With his discrimination ripening through many a
long life, the man of wisdom makes me his refuge
– knows that Vasudeva (Brahman) is all there is.
How rare is such a great one!*

∽

THE sage Ashtavakra tells us what bondage is
and what liberation is. He says, "It means bondage
when the mind desires something or grieves at
something; it means liberation when the mind
does not desire or grieve, does not accept or reject,
does not feel happy or unhappy." Now, the human
mind, trained and conditioned as it is, is incapable
of realising that the non-desiring includes desiring
the knowledge of your true nature: desire does
not mean only desiring some object but includes

the desire for freedom from bondage. Wherever there is desire there must be the individual "me" doing the desiring, and therefore "bondage".

Ashtavakra also says: "It means bondage when the mind is attached to any sense experience; it is liberation when the mind is detached from all sense experience." The mind is the "me" who is attached to sense experiences.

How does the "me", the personal identification arise? In the process of manifestation and its functioning – for this God's game or *lila* to take place – for the love and hate relationships to arise, Consciousness (or God) identifies itself with each individual organism, and creates the "me" who desires or grieves for something, who attaches himself to the same experiences. When there is the sudden realization that this "me" is only a concept which does not really exist, the identification with the organism as a separate entity, disappears.

Lord Krishna says that this process of the creation of the "me" and its destruction, which means liberation from the bondage of identification and attachment, takes many lifetimes.

Ultimately there is the sudden realization that all there is, is Consciousness, that all that

has happened, and is happening, and will happen
is because of God's Will and not because of
the efforts of the fictitious "me". This sudden
realization, itself because of God's Will as God's
Grace, means enlightenment or awakening.

∿

अन्तकाले च मामेव स्मरन्मुक्त्वा कलेवरम् ।
य:प्रयाति स मद्भावं याति नास्त्ययत्र संशय: ॥

*If at the time of death, when a man drops his body,
he departs with his consciousness absorbed in Me
alone, he will be united with My being – there is
no doubt about this.*

∽

THE Taoist sage Huang-Po has an interesting
statement which has context to this verse. Huang
Po says:

"If an ordinary man, when he is about to die,
could only see the five elements of consciousness as
void; the four physical elements as not constituting
a "me"; the real Mind as form-less and neither
coming nor going; his nature as something
neither commencing at his birth nor perishing
at his death, but as whole and motionless in its

very depths; his Mind and environmental objects as One – if he could really have this happen, he would receive enlightenment in a flash. He would no longer be entangled by the Triple World: he would be a world transcender...If he should behold the glorious sight of all the Buddhas coming to welcome him, surrounded by every kind of gorgeous manifestation, he would feel no desire to approach them. If he should behold all sorts of horrific forms surrounding him, he would experience no terror. He would just be himself, oblivious of conceptual thought, and one with the absolute. This is the fundamental principle."

∾

परस्तस्मात्तुभावोऽन्य: अव्यक्तोऽव्यक्तात्सनातन: ।
य: स सर्वेषु भूतेषु नश्यत्सु न विनश्यति ॥

अव्यक्तोऽक्षर इत्युक्त: तमाहु: परमां गतिम् ।
यं प्राप्य न निवर्तन्ते तद्धाम परमं मम ॥

*Behind the manifest and the unmanifest (which
concerns phenomenality) there is another
Noumenal awareness which is eternal and
changeless – this is not dissolved in the general
cosmic dissolution. This imperishable Unmanifest
Awareness is said to be the highest state of Being.
Those who reach It do not return.*

ॐ

SAINT Jnaneshwar in his *Anubhavamrita*
(Experience of Immortality) refers to this point:
the arising of consciousness – I Am – on the

original state of the plenum or pure potentiality when awareness was not aware of itself. It is only when the sense of presence – I Am – arises on the original primal state of unicity that consciousness concurrently comes into movement and brings forth upon itself the totality of manifestation. The movement of consciousness also simultaneously brings about the concepts of knowledge, *vidya* (I am – the sense of impersonal presence) and ignorance, *avidya* (when the impersonal consciousness or presence becomes identified with each sentient being as a separate entity). The unicity of the potential plenum – the I-subject – gets dichotomized in the process of manifestation as subject and object, each object considering itself as the pseudo-subject observer vis-a-vis all other observed objects. This itself – the individual entitification – is the conceptual "bondage" of the individual as a separate entity. And "liberation" consists in the realization that our true nature is the impersonal consciousness (I am That; That thou art) and not the individual body-mind organism with which consciousness had identified itself. When such a realization – the transformation or *paravritti* – occurs, the pseudo-subject ceases to be an object and becomes void by the superimposition of the opposites (subject/object) over each other; and through this void or nothingness, the pseudo-subject returns to the original subjectivity which is the potential plenum.

Jnaneshwar explains that the Absolute-Noumenon-Subject cannot be an object to itself or anyone else, and this is the very reason for its primal beingness. It is the eternal subject – the substratum – which manifests itself objectively by extending itself in conceptual space-time so that it may become perceptible as phenomenal objects. This total potentiality – The I-subject – cannot offer itself for comprehension because it would then be an object. The eye can see everything else but it cannot see itself!

❧

राजविद्या राजगुह्यं पवित्रमिदमुत्तमम् ।
प्रत्यक्षावगमं धर्म्यं सुसुखं कर्तुमव्ययम् ॥

मया ततमिदं सर्वं जगदव्यक्तमूर्तिना ।
मत्स्थानि सर्वभूतानि न चाहं तेष्ववस्थित: ॥

This is the knowledge above all other, the sovereign secret, the ultimate purifier. Its virtue is great, its practice relatively easy, and it is made plain only to the eye of the mystic. Thus is man brought to the Truth eternal.

The entire universe is pervaded by Me in that eternal form of mine which is not manifest to the senses. Although I am not within any creature (physically), all creatures exist within me.

॰

LORD Krishna, in this verse, calls Advaita as the sovereign knowledge, the sovereign secret by which man is brought to the ultimate, eternal Truth. Self-Enquiry is relatively easy because it does not entail any formal observance of any physical and mental discipline for a prescribed period of time: It can be apprehended directly by an immediate experience of the Self, and once this is experienced directly, the sense of personal doership, the "me" is totally annihilated for all time.

This sovereign method is a great purifier because it does not entail any strenuous disciplines and yet it internally purifies the seeker. It is, however, not available to all: it is made plain only to the eye of the mystic, only to those who have the receptivity to this teaching. Those whose nature inclines them towards seeking material gain or power will not even be interested in seeking the Self.

This teaching (that the entire universe is pervaded by Him in that eternal form not manifest to the senses) is thus not available to those whose *dharma*, whose set of natural characteristics, does not permit them to be open to this teaching. As Saint Jnaneshwar has put it, this teaching will be available only to him who is able to see his face without the aid of the mirror!

Finally, Lord Krishna says in this verse that He is not within any creature but that all creatures exist within Him. In this one line, Lord Krishna expresses the simultaneous principles of immanence and transcendence. All creatures are part of the reflection or manifest expression of the unmanifest: the unmanifest therefore is immanent in all creatures but, at the same time, the unmanifest transcends all creation. The substance can exist without the shadow but the shadow cannot exist without the substance: the substance, therefore, is immanent in the shadow, and at the same time, transcends the shadow.

∿

यो मामजमनादिं च वेत्ति लोकमहेश्वरम्।
असंमूढ: स मर्त्येषु सर्वपापै: प्रमुच्यते ॥

*The one who knows Me as being birthless, without
beginning, Lord of the universe, he alone among
mortals is stainless of sin, unvexed by delusion.*

∾

"THE one who knows Me" refers not to
someone who thinks he believes in God (or in the
Impersonal Noumenon) who is immanent in the
manifest universe, at the same time, transcending
it. The knowing means a total and in-depth
apprehension – a total faith – in God, not just a
pious belief in God.

Such in-depth apprehension means a total faith
that all that happens is God's Will, that no human
being can have his own free will to be master of
his own destiny. This also means an acceptance –

a total acceptance – of whatever God does in His infinite wisdom, without any judging according to one's own standards of fair play! You will be judging not the body-mind organism through which God's action has been created, but God himself if you judge anything that happens in the world according to your standards.

Ramakrishna Paramahaunsa said, "Be absolutely certain totally accept – that you are a machine which is operated upon by God, and then do whatever you like!" Whatever you like at any time will be strictly according to the natural characteristics with which God has endowed your organism. So, whatever you like at any time and do it, must necessarily be part of God's action, irrespective of the fact that you think it is your action. If you truly accept that all actions are God's actions, how can you even involve yourself with the concept of "sin"? It is precisely from this point of view that Lord Krishna says, "he alone among mortals (who is full of conviction that everything happens by God's Will) is stainless of sin," unvexed by delusion – the delusion of a sense of personal doership.

∾

तेषां सततयुक्तानां भजतां प्रीतिपूर्वकम् ।
ददामि बुद्धियोगं तं येन मामुपयान्ति ते ॥

तेषामेवानुकम्पार्थ अहमज्ञानजं तमः ।
नाशयाम्यात्मभावस्थः ज्ञानदीपेन भास्वता ॥

To them, always aware of their Lord, and ever devoted, the strength and depth of their devotion brings forth from Me the Yoga of discrimination which illumines and guides them towards Me.

By the grace of My compassion, there in the ignorant heart where I dwell, I become the brilliant lamp of knowledge, dispelling the darkness of ignorance.

ॐ

IT is normally not possible for the human being whose natural inclination is love and devotion to

God – the *Bhakti* path – to apprehend directly the sovereign secret to which Lord Krishna has referred in verse IX 2 – the ultimate purifier. So He says in these two verses that when the devotion of the devotees reaches great intensity – and only the devotion and love to God remains, without even the individuality of the devotee – then He instils in them the necessary receptivity – the *Buddhi-yoga*, the *Yoga* of discrimination – which leads them to the direct experience of the Imperishable Self, the ultimate purifier when the sense of personal doership is totally annihilated.

To be a seeker is itself a matter of God's Grace, and the further progress in the process is also a matter of God's Grace.

When the dark ignorance is destroyed by the lamp of knowledge though the *Buddhi-yoga*, the *Yoga* of knowledge and discrimination, the self stands revealed in its own glory as the One-without-a-second, all pervading in its fullness. This ultimate happening is entirely a matter of God's Grace and not something achievable by the devotee through his own efforts.

❧

अहमात्मा गुडाकेश सर्वभूताशयस्थित: ।
अहमादिश्च मध्यं च भूतानामन्त एवच ॥

I am the Atman *that dwells in the heart of every mortal creature: I am the beginning, I am the life-span, and I am the end of all beings.*

∽

THIS is the central theme of the *Bhagavad Gita*, and Lord Krishna states this in forceful terms.

The meaning is very clear and is one of the verses on which meditation could be based with much success.

∽

कालोऽस्मि लोकक्षयकृत्प्रवृद्ध: ।
लोकान् समाहर्तुमिह प्रवृत्त: ॥
ऋतेऽपि त्वां न भविष्यन्ति सर्वे ।
येऽवस्थिता: प्रत्यनीकेषु योद्धा: ॥

तस्मात्त्वमुत्तिष्ठ यशो लभस्व ।
जित्वा शत्रून् भुङ्क्ष्व राज्यं समृद्धम् ॥
मयैवैते निहता: पूर्वमेव ।
निमित्तमात्रं भव सव्यसाचिन् ॥

I am come as Time, the ultimate waster of the people, ready for the hour that ripens to their doom. The warriors, arrayed in hostile armies facing each other, shall not live, whether you strike or stay your hand.

Therefore, arise and fight. Win kingdom, wealth and glory. Merely be the apparent instrument for their end – they have already been slain by Me – O, ambidextrous bowman.

EVERYTHING that is born or created must end – this is the law of nature, and in the process, human beings become the apparent reasons and instruments. In fact they have nothing to do other than being mere instruments: they have no free will or choice. In this verse, Lord Krishna tells Arjuna that although Arjuna thinks in terms of himself being the killer and, the enemies, the ones he would kill, actually He as Time has already killed them. There is no need for Arjuna to feel any regret, Arjuna's unhappiness stems from his feeling of personal doership, and here again, the Lord reminds Arjuna that never can he be anything but an apparent instrument for anything that happens as part of the functioning of Totality. In subtle terms, the Lord tells Arjuna not to question the functioning of Totality, to enjoy the "kingdom, wealth and glory" that is his destiny – never forgetting that these too will be subject to the ultimate demolition and annihilation due to the efflux of Time.

"I am Time" says Krishna. That is to say, Time is a concept as part of the concept of space-time which came along with the manifestation on the arising of Consciousness. For manifestation to happen, the concept of space is necessary for the objects to be constructed; Time is necessary for these manifested objects to be observed. In other words, Space-Time is a necessary adjunct of manifestation as such.

∾

श्रेयो हि ज्ञानमभ्यासात् ज्ञानाद्ध्यानं विशिष्यते ।
ध्यानात्कर्मफलत्यागः त्यागाच्छान्तिरनन्तरम् ॥

*Concentration, practised with discernment, is
certainly better than the mechanical repetition of
a ritual or a prayer. Absorption in God throughout
the day – keeping Him in your heart always –
is even better than concentration. But, above
all, renunciation – the shedding of the sense of
doership and of the expectation of the fruits of
action – brings instant peace to the spirit.*

෩

EVERY seeker, at one time or another, is
plagued by the question as to which spiritual
practice he should follow. He does not realize
that actually he does not have the free will to
choose any particular spiritual practice: he must
have the natural tendency towards that particular
practice, otherwise the effort would be wasted.

Nevertheless, the question remains about which practice is the best. Here Lord Krishna gives the answer.

It may be that a particular aspirant, for various reasons and circumstances, is only able to repeat continuously for a certain length of time a particular ritual or a prayer. Even that, in the circumstances, would be good enough – better than nothing – because, as the Lord has stressed in an earlier verse, no spiritual practice can ever be wasted. But instead of mere mechanical repetition, if there is a certain concentration of the mind, it would be even better. Better than concentration would be absorption in God throughout the day. "Absorption in God throughout the day" does not mean to the exclusion of all other activity, which would be most impractical. What is meant is that you should keep Him in your heart always: this means a true conviction that all there is, is God or Totality, which prevails all the time. But above all, says the Lord, the shedding of the sense of doership is ultimately the absolute necessity. So long as there is a sense of personal doership – I am doing the practice of repeating the prayer, I am invoking God or I am doing the meditation – the practice would be of a lower order. Only when there is the deepest conviction that all there is, is Consciousness – that only God's Will prevails and there can be no personal will or effort – only then will peace prevail.

❧

उपद्रष्टानुमन्ता च भर्ता भोक्ता महेश्वर: ।
परमात्मेति चाप्युक्त: देहेऽस्मिन्पुरूष पर: ॥

य एवं वेत्ति पुरूषं प्रकृतिं च गुणै: सह ।
सर्वथा वर्तमानोऽपि न स भूयोऽभिजायते ॥

The supreme Brahman – Purusha – *in the body is also called the Witness. He makes all our actions happen, sanctions them as it were, experiencing all our experiences. He is the infinite Being, the supreme* Atman.

He who has experienced this Purusha, *the* Brahman, *directly and realized It as none other than* Prakriti *and the* gunas, *will not be reborn, irrespective of how he has lived his life.*

❧

NOUMENON and the phenomena, the

unmanifest and the manifested universe, *Shiva* and *Shakti*, *Purusha* and *Prakriti*, are what might be called the parents of the universe, the original interrelated or polaric opposites – the one conceives the total potential and the other the totality of what is sensorially perceptible. The important point is that they are only apparently different but that they include each other and, as such, are not really different. They are the opposite aspects of what would remain in their mutual negation of what is conceived – THAT which is prior to the conceiving process, or prior to the arising of Consciousness. Take away all that appears to be, all that is sensorially perceptible, all that is an effective reaction like likes and dislikes – and all that remains is pure subjectivity without any trace of objectivity.

As Saint Jnaneshwar has put it, apart from these two, nothing exists in this world; and as *Purusha* is asleep, it is only *Prakriti* that is active in the world, and is in charge of the working of the world, just as the housewife takes charge of the household in the absence of the husband. The husband, however, is aware of what is going on – as the Witness.

In other words, the entire multiplicity of phenomena in this world has no existence on its own because they are only an appearance in the consciousness-in-movement. When the consciousness-in-movement forgets its universal or impersonal nature (*Purusha* is asleep), and proceeds to identity itself with each of the many sentient objects, the sentient object assumes a pseudo-subjectivity and a sense of doership (takes charge of the working of the world).

Jnaneshwar further goes on to explain:

These two – *Shiva* and *Shakti* – find their oneness in their original unicity and acquire their duality only for the sake of the conceptual manifestation. These two become subject and object to each other, but both are subjectivity in their unicity. The difference between *Shiva* and *Shakti* is merely in name and form, they are of the same essential "substance". The duality in the world is only notional – like similar fragrance out of two flowers from the same plant or the same sight from the two eyes.

It is interesting to note the remarks of Ramakrishna Paramahaunsa in this respect:

The universe has come into being as a result of

the union between the *Purusha* and the *Prakriti*.
The master of the family is seated somewhere
absorbed in thought. The housewife busies herself
and attends to all the details of the household
affairs. Now and then she acquaints her husband
with what is taking place and seeks his counsel
when necessary. The husband approves of what
has taken place and suggests what should happen
next. It is in this way that the *Purusha* and *Prakriti*
function.

When this position is deeply apprehended,
says Lord Krishna, the process of awakening is
complete and needs no other lives for completion,
in addition to the body-mind organism through
which this final awakening has taken place.

Again, it is interesting to note the remarks, in
this context, of Ramakrishna Paramahaunsa:

When the unburnt pots get damaged, the
potter makes new pots out of them. But when a
pot burnt in the kiln breaks, the broken pieces are
no longer required. Similarly a life in ignorance
needs another life (for further processing). But
that man whose *Karma* is burnt out by the fire of
knowledge has completed the process. He enters
the Absolute.

प्रकृत्यैव च कर्माणि क्रियमाणानि सर्वश: ।
य: पश्यति तथात्मानं अकर्तारं स पश्यति ॥

यदा भूतपृथग्भावं एकस्थमनुपश्यति ।
तत एव च विस्तारं ब्रह्म संपद्यते तदा ॥

अनादित्वान्निर्गुणत्वात् परमात्मायमव्यय: ।
शरीरस्थोऽपि कौन्तेय न करोति न लिप्यते ॥

*That man truly sees who perceives all actions
performed by all body-mind organisms as having
happened because of* Prakriti. *He sees the* Atman
as being actionless.

*He who sees the entire variety of beings as resting
in the One, united in* Brahman, *brought forth in
evolution from* Brahman *alone, finds* Brahman
himself.

The infinite Atman, *without beginning, beyond the gunas, is not subject to change and is imperishable.*

Therefore, though It dwells in body (as its life-force), It neither acts nor is tainted by the actions or their consequences.

THESE verses are important but self-explanatory, and need no elaboration.

∾

देवी संपद्विमोक्षाय निबन्धायासुरी मता।
मा शुच: संपदं दैवीं अभिजातोऽसि पाण्डव॥

The birthright of the divine nature leads to liberation; the birthright of the demonic nature leads to greater bondage. Grieve not, O Arjuna, your birthright is divine.

∾

THE process from the total identification with the body-mind organism as a separate entity with free will and independence of action – a selfish and totally self-centred individual – to the total disidentification with the organism due to the unequivocal acceptance of God's Will in everything that happens, a conviction that the individual organism is merely an instrument at the total disposal of God's Will – this process is a long and arduous one. And the fact remains that this process itself is an impersonal one in which the individual as a mere instrument, has no freedom of action. The totality of this situation makes one fearful of knowing where one stands in this long and arduous process.

Arjuna is precisely in this situation, and the good Lord, fully conscious of this fact, hastens to assure Arjuna that he has no cause to be despondent. The very fact that he is a seeker after Truth – which is itself God's Grace – should assure him that his "birthright is divine": he is well ahead in the phenomenal process from the darkness of ignorance to the light of true knowledge.

∾

सत्त्वानुरूपा सर्वस्य श्रद्धा भवति भारत ।
श्रद्धामयोऽयं पुरूष: यो यच्छ्द्ध: स एव स: ॥

*The faith of each individual is in accordance with
his natural temperament. The man is indeed no
different from the faith itself. Whatever his faith
is, he is.*

∾

EVERY human organism is conceived and
created with certain given characteristics: physical,
mental, intellectual, temperamental. No person
has any choice or control concerning his parents
and, therefore, in what environmental conditions
he would be born. In other words, no person has
any choice over his genes-DNA; nor does he have
any choice over the conditioning he would get in
the environment in which he is born. Therefore,
it is a fact that he has no choice over either his
genes or his environmental conditioning. And

the DNA plus the conditioning is the basic cause of a person's personality, his psyche, based on his natural characteristics as developed by the environmental conditioning. His "faith", his outlook on life and living, will therefore also be based on these factors.

This "faith" will make a person behave in accordance with his natural characteristics. In other words, a human being is a programmed instrument at the will of God. If God wants to produce a certain action through a particular human organism, all he has to do is to send an impulse, a thought or a feeling, or, he has to make the organism see something, or hear something or smell something – and the brain will react to the outside impulse or event strictly according to the natural characteristics, according to the man's "faith". This natural reaction of the programmed organism is usually considered by an individual as *his* action. Thus, whatever the faith is, the individual is.

❧

न हि देहभृता शक्यं त्यक्तुं कर्माण्यशेषत: ।
यस्तु कर्मफलत्यागी स त्यागीत्यभिधीयते ॥

It is indeed impossible for an embodied being to renounce action entirely, but he who has renounced the fruits of action is said to be truly non-attached.

∽

IN this verse, Lord Krishna clearly brings out the difference between renunciation of action and renunciation of the fruits of action.

The word "renunciation" usually means for the average person, renouncing, giving up action. But giving up action is an impossibility because the energy within the organism will not allow the organism to remain idle for any length of time. Even if a *Yogi* went into *samadhi*, the energy within will bring him back to earth some time or the other.

The one who is truly non-attached is the one who is not concerned with the fruits of actions. And the ordinary person, fully identified with the organism as a separate entity with independence of choice and action, would never be able to renounce the fruits of action and he would consider himself entitled to the fruits of his action.

The only way the renunciation of the fruits of action can happen is when the deepest intuitive understanding happens that no action can ever be the individual's action, that all actions are in fact reactions of the body-mind organism to the outside impulse according to its natural characteristics.

❧

यस्य नाहंकृतो भाव: बुद्धिर्यस्य न लिप्यते ।
हत्वाऽपि स इमॉल्लोकान् न हन्ति न निबध्यते ॥

*No act will create any bondage for him, whose mind
is free of attachment and whose understanding
is untainted by the ego. Although he slay these
thousands, he does not kill, nor is he bound by
the action.*

∾

LORD Krishna repeatedly assures Arjuna that
he will attract sin for actions only if he assumes
doership for those acts, but that if he should be
truly convinced and approached the truth that his
enemies have already been slain by the Lord in his
capacity as almighty Time, and that he, Arjuna,
would only be an apparent cause and instrument
in their death, then no possible taint of sin would
accrue to him.

In this verse again, he reiterates the same
point.

सर्वभूतेषु येनैकं भावमव्ययमीक्षते ।
अविभक्तं विभक्तेषु तज्ज्ञानं विद्धि सात्त्विकम् ॥

That knowledge is sattvika *(pure), by which the
one Imperishable Being, the deathless, is seen in
all existences in the midst of all the diversity.*

ॐ

WHAT has appeared as manifestation is
merely a kind of reflection of the basic ground
– call it Consciousness-at-rest, God or whatever.
Seeing the oneness not only in the immense variety
in the manifestation but between the manifest
and the unmanifest is what is really meant by
enlightenment or awakening.

Once the individual forgets this oneness
– not only between the manifestation as in its
diversity, but also between the manifest and the
unmanifest – then he begins to think in terms of

his individuality and his personal security. Once he begins to think in terms of personal security, he creates any number of problems for himself. So, at that level the first step in understanding the nature of the human being would be that there can be no such thing as security for the individual, that movement and change are the very basis of life and living. This understanding is the basis of understanding life, to go back into the impersonality of life, in which the individual is merely an instrument.

Such understanding is *sattvika* or pure knowledge.

∾

नियतं सङ्‌रहितं अरागद्वेषत: कृतम् ।
अफलप्रेप्सुना कर्म यत्तत्सात्त्विकमुच्यते ॥

That action is said to be sattvika, *which is spontaneous and natural, done without attachment, neither for pleasure nor out of compulsion, by one who is not concerned with the fruit of the action. Such an action is called* sattvika.

∾

THE previous verse explained what knowledge was *sattvika* or pure. In this verse is explained what action is considered *sattvika* or pure: that action is pure in which there is no sense of personal doership, and in which there is no concern for the reward of the action. When there is no concern for the consequences of the action because there is no personal involvement, there is neither a sense of achievement if the action is successful, nor a sense of guilt or failure if the action is not considered successful.

Such an attitude is possible only if there is the full realization that any action which a person considers his or her action is in fact only a reaction of the organism to an outside impulse – be it a thought, or something seen or something heard or whatever – and that such reaction is based entirely on the natural characteristics of that particular organism. In other words, such an attitude is possible only if there is the deepest conviction that the individual human being is merely an instrument through which God brings about such action as He thinks fit according to the destiny of that organism, and the Universal Plan.

One is again reminded of Shri Ramakrishna Paramahaunsa's declaration: "Be totally convinced that you are merely a machine that is operated upon by God, and then you may do whatever you like."

❧

श्रेयान्स्वधर्मो विगुण: परधर्मात्स्वनुष्ठितात्।
स्वभावनियतं कर्म कुर्वन्नाप्नोति किल्बिषम्॥

Better is one's own dharma though imperfect,
than the dharma of another better performed. He
who does the duty ordained by his own nature
incurs no sin.

ೲ

HERE again, Lord Krishna impresses upon
Arjuna the importance of realizing that ultimately
it is one's own nature – one's own *dharma* –
that will prevail. To try to go against nature is
dangerous. To act accordingly to one's nature – to
accept that whatever happens is the will of God –
is to go with the flow. To swim against the current
is both difficult and hazardous, though at first it
might seem to be a better course.

The Lord further assures Arjuna that even
if the consequences of one's action seem to be

injurious to others – and the consequences to the organism may seem unfortunate – the basic fact remains that if there was no personal sense of doership involved, there would be no question of incurring any sin.

∾

यदहङ्कारमाश्रित्य न योत्स्य इति मन्यसे ।
मिथ्यैष व्यवसायस्ते प्रकृतिस्त्वां नियोक्ष्यति ॥

स्वभावजेन कौन्तेय निबद्धः स्वेन कर्मणा ।
कर्तुनेच्छसि यन्मोहात् करिष्यस्यवशोऽपि तत् ॥

ईश्वरः सर्वभूतानां हृद्देशेऽर्जुन तिष्ठति ।
भ्रामयन्सर्वभूतानि यन्त्रारूढानि मायया ॥

तमेव शरणं गच्छ सर्वभावेन भारत ।
तत्प्रसादात्परां शान्ति स्थानं प्राप्स्यसि शाश्वतम् ॥

*If, in your vanity, you decide not to fight, your
resolve would be in vain: your own nature will
drive you to the act.*

*Bound by your own Karma born of your nature,
you will do that very thing which your ignorance*

seeks to avoid.

The Lord lives in the heart of every creature. By His Maya He causes all beings to wander through life as though mounted on a machine.

Take refuge utterly in Him. By His Grace, you will gain supreme peace and reach the Eternal Abode.

∾

THESE verses are self-explanatory and need no elaboration.

∾

Chapter XVIII / 66

सर्वधर्मान्परित्यज्य मामेकं शरणं व्रज ।
अहं त्वा सर्वपापेभ्य: मोक्षयिष्यामि मा शुच: ॥

Surrender all your duties to Me – take refuge in Me. Fear no longer. I will save you from sin and bondage.

॰

THIS verse is one of the most well-known, and at the same time one of the most controversial, in the entire *Bhagavad Gita*. The controversy centres around the interpretation of the first line "*sarva dharman parityajya*" (abandoning all *dharmas*). The word "*dharma*" is used in the *Gita* in a number of ways, and thus the controversy. This is unfortunate because the really meaningful term is "surrender to me". Abandoning all *dharmas* simply means abandoning all concepts.

The state of self-surrender – or the act of taking refuge in the Lord – is one and the same for the

Yogi, the *bhakta* and the *jnani*: the *Yogi* merges in the *sat* aspect of the Reality – *sat-chit-ananda*; the *jnani* waxes as the *chit*, and the *bhakta* blooms in the *ananda* aspect. The main point is that the sense of personal individuality as an independent entity (with choice of decision and action) has to disappear.

The essence of this verse, one of those at the very end, would appear to be to anticipate the final query from Arjuna, who would obviously be confused by the many things he has been told.

Arjuna's final query would obviously be: "O Lord, you have deigned to tell me so many things in so many different ways in order to show me the Truth, but, frankly, I am confused. Please do tell me, in brief terms, what I should do, how I should act in life."

From this point of view, the verse could be paraphrased as under:

"Forget all you have heard, and remember only one thing: Consciousness – or God – is all there is, permeating the smallest particle in the universe. How should you act in this world? Just be totally convinced that you are only an instrument or machine that God operates in order

115

to bring about such actions as He considers fit. A true conviction of this means a true surrender to Me. Surrender to Me in this manner, and then you may act any way you want and live any way you like."

❦